Mary Angeline Hallock

The Child's History of King Solomon

Mary Angeline Hallock

The Child's History of King Solomon

ISBN/EAN: 9783337318581

Printed in Europe, USA, Canada, Australia, Japan

Cover: Foto ©ninafisch / pixelio.de

More available books at **www.hansebooks.com**

THE CHILD'S HISTORY

OF

KING SOLOMON.

BY MRS. M. A. HALLOCK,

AUTHOR OF "THAT SWEET STORY OF OLD," "CHILD'S HISTORY OF PAUL," ETC.

"My son, keep thy father's commandment, and forsake not the law of thy mother."
PROVERBS 6 : 20.

PUBLISHED BY THE
AMERICAN TRACT SOCIETY,
150 NASSAU-STREET, NEW YORK.

ENTERED according to Act of Congress, in the year 1869, by the AMERICAN TRACT SOCIETY, in the Clerk's Office of the District Court of the United States for the Southern District of New York.

CONTENTS.

CHAPTER I.
Solomon's Birth—The Brilliant Crown .... PAGE 7

CHAPTER II.
Absalom's Return and Rebellion 17

CHAPTER III.
Adonijah's Revolt—Solomon crowned 28

CHAPTER IV.
David assembles the People, and gives a Charge to Solomon 37

CHAPTER V.
Solomon at Gibeon—His Wise Choice—He judges between the Two Mothers 47

CHAPTER VI.
The Dedication—Solomon's Palace 61

died. Perhaps the young who read this may remember how sad David was while that child was so sick; how he fasted and prayed, and lay on the ground all night. But God would not hear his prayer, because he had done a very wicked thing and must be punished; and when the child had pined away for a week God took his soul, and his little body was cold and stiff in death.

The servants hardly dared tell David that the child was gone, for fear of increasing his sorrow; but when he heard it, he felt that God was just and good, and he changed his clothes, and went into the house of the Lord and worshipped. After that, he returned home and broke his long fast with some food.

David prayed for the child as long as it was alive, but no longer. There are some people who think it right to pray for the dead; so they pay the priests large sums of money to make long prayers, hoping that their deceased friends will be the happier for it. David knew better, and arose from his lowly posture before the Lord as soon as he learned that his child was gone.

God saw that David was very sorry for his sin, and as a token of his pardon gave him another son, whom he called SOLOMON. This was not, however, his only name, for he had been but a few days with his parents, when Nathan, the prophet of the Lord, came to the palace to see him. This was the same man whom God had sent to tell David that the other child should die. And now, as David saw him approaching, he may have feared that he was about to announce again something distressing. But Nathan had no such tidings, for he looked kindly upon the babe, and said, "His name shall be *Jedidiah*," a name which means, "Beloved of the Lord." God loved Solomon even then, before he was old enough to know whether he was doing right or wrong. And does he not love all little children? Christ blessed them when he was upon earth, and they may be blessed both here and hereafter, if they love and obey the God who made them, and the Saviour who redeemed them.

Solomon's mother was very beautiful, so the Bible says; and we hope that she was also good and kind, for she was to have the training of her child, while his father who was a great warrior was engaged in subduing the wicked nations around him.

At the time of Solomon's birth, David had an army under Joab his nephew, at a place on the east side of Jordan, where they were sent to subdue the Ammonites. The war had been in progress two or three years, and was the one in which Uriah, Bathsheba's first husband, perished. One day a messenger from Joab came to Jerusalem, who told David that the Ammonites were nearly conquered, and were then shut up in Rabbah, their royal city, and that Joab wished him to come with more troops, and take the city himself, and have the honor of the conquest. David immediately left

Jerusalem with an army, and after several days of weary march, arrived at Rabbah, which he attacked and conquered. The king of the Ammonites was found in the city, dressed in his royal robes, and wearing upon his head a crown sparkling with precious stones, the weight or worth of which was a talent of gold. David took it from the monarch's head, and placing it upon his own, returned with his army and captives in triumph to Jerusalem. Solomon was too young at that time to notice the glittering crown of his father; but his six half-brothers, Amnon, Chileab, Absalom, Adonijah, Shephatiah, and Ithream, undoubtedly gathered around it with admiring wonder; each, perhaps, looking forward in his own mind to the hoped-for time when he should have it set upon his own head, and become a king among the nations. David never lost a battle, and the crown undoubtedly remained in the family, and probably in after years graced the head of Solomon himself.

David had six wives besides Bathsheba, each of whom had one son, and we can easily imagine that there were some strifes and envyings in that family circle. Indeed, we find that the boys grew up with wild and ungovernable passions, which caused David their father much grief. Besides his own sons, he had a nephew, his brother's son, in his family, an unprincipled young man, full of worldly wisdom and craftiness, whose name was Jonadab.

This wily fellow flattered the king's sons, and secretly instilled principles into their minds calculated to work their ruin. To Amnon, the eldest, and heir apparent to the throne, he was particularly attentive, and apparently kind: he took him warmly into his heart, called him his "friend," and revealed to him his most secret and wicked designs. Jonadab saw that he was fast getting Amnon under his power, and intimated to him one day that as he was the son of a king, he should be indulged in every wish, whether good or bad, and offered his services in the accomplishment of his wishes. Amnon, like many other young men since his day, yielded to bad advice, and secured his own ruin. A family difficulty arose, in which Amnon became very guilty, and for which Absalom determined to kill him.

Chileab was probably dead, as no further mention is made of him; and as another motive for the proposed murder, Absalom may have thought, through this step, to reach his father's throne. These six sons were born before the end of David's seven years' residence at Hebron, and were all probably in the prime of early manhood, and each had a dwelling and interests of his own.

Amnon accepted an invitation to Absalom's house one day, and entered joyfully into the pleasures of a feast; but when he was nearly drunk with the wine which had been supplied for that very purpose, the fatal blow was given by Absalom's

14   THE HISTORY OF KING SOLOMON.

command, and Amnon lay a corpse at the feet of his brother. Jonadab had not been invited, for he was no favorite with Absalom; and when word reached the king that all his sons were slain, Jonadab saw the truth at once, and told his uncle that he was confident that Amnon alone was dead, for he had observed in Absalom a secret hatred towards him for two years past. This proved true;

one son was dead, and another was a murderer, fleeing from his father's presence; and David tore his garments, lay upon the ground, and wept bitterly. The consequences of his own sins, and his over indulgence to his children were beginning to show themselves; and it humbled him before God, and helped to qualify him, we may hope, to discharge with faithfulness his duties towards his little boy Solomon. Some years had gone by since he had been added to the family, and he had learned, in his childish innocence, to love them all. Absalom, his tall, handsome brother, who had probably often entered into his sports and humored him in his childish preferences, had gone, and a dreadful deed had been committed which deeply grieved his beloved father; and although Solomon could not fully comprehend the nature of the crime, his young heart undoubtedly sympathized deeply in the sorrow of those around him. So little children often suffer in consequence of the sins of others.

David learned that Absalom had crossed the river Jordan, and gone on east to his grandfather, who was king of Geshur; and it was his duty to recall and punish him, according to the laws of God

But his own strong love for Absalom revolted at the idea, and Maacah, Absalom's mother, used all her influence to have her father, the king of Geshur, shield his grandson from harm; and so Absalom went unpunished. But God saw his wickedness, and had an eye upon him, for he remembers all our sins.

We should all rejoice that Christ, our dear Saviour, has died for us, and made it possible for God to forgive our iniquities; for it is only through him that any are pardoned and saved.

CHAPTER II.

Absalom's Return and Rebellion.

THREE years went by after Absalom left home, during which time Solomon became old enough to begin to receive that instruction and discipline which was to fit him to become a wise king, at the head of a great and powerful nation; and we may believe that his father **spared no** pains in his training. David, however, could **not forget his** beloved Absalom, **and** longed **to go and bring him** home: but this he could **not do without seeming** to countenance **his** guilt; and he remained inactive till Joab, **his** nephew and general, succeeded by artifice in bringing the thing about.

At length **David told J**oab to go, and after some days of absence he returned with Absalom. The king, however, refused to allow him to come into his presence, and Joab, at the king's command, took Absalom to his former home. This was very galling to the guilty young man, and he determined to bring about a change by some means or other. He was far from being penitent for any thing he had done, and in a pert and commanding way, he sent word to Joab to come to him, intending to send him to his father to secure an interview. Joab paid no attention to these messages, which so much provoked Absalom that he ordered his servants to set on fire a field of barley belonging to Joab, expecting that this, if nothing else, would bring him to his house.

Joab heard that his field of grain was entirely destroyed, and went over to complain about it, when Absalom demanded of him to see the king; and Joab, having interests of his own to subserve, used his influence with David, and Absalom was finally brought into the palace, where he prostrated

ABSALOM'S RETURN AND REBELLION.

himself to the ground before his father. David, with a heart full of love and pity, raised and kissed this treacherous son.

Absalom had now gained one point; and then he set himself to work to draw away the hearts of the people from his father, which he soon in no small degree accomplished; for, united to his pleasant address and wily tact, "there was none in Israel to be so much praised for beauty as he; from the crown of his head to the sole of his foot, there was no blemish in him:" and beauty then, as well as since, had no small influence with the world.

Absalom now commenced riding through the city in his chariot, with fifty men running before him, like a king already in power; and had not his father been blinded by partiality, he would have seen the secret intentions of his designing son.

Solomon was not far from eight years old, when word reached his father that Absalom had planned a revolt, and was then marching with a strong force towards the city; and he must have participated

ABSALOM'S RETURN AND REBELLION.

largely in the distress that filled the palace. David immediately gathered his wives and children, and such effects as his servants could carry, and accompanied by his old body-guard of six hundred men, and by his most devoted friends, left the city. Passing down from the east gate into the valley of the Kidron, the men and women, with Bathsheba and Solomon, went over the brook, and followed the king as he ascended, barefoot, the Mount of Olives. David felt that he was under the rebuke of the Lord, and wept as he went; the people also covered their heads and followed weeping, and all the country through which they passed wept with a loud voice.

Passing onward, they had a long and weary march through a rugged and desolate region, to the bank of the river Jordan: the men were in great straits, the women distressed and in tears, while the children were no doubt hungry and tired. It was almost night when they stopped to refresh themselves, and soon after, a messenger arrived, who advised the king and his men to move across the Jordan as quickly as possible, as Absalom might come upon them before morning, and find them defenceless. They immediately commenced the work, and during the night, by some means, although they had no bridge, they were all transported across the water, and were comparatively safe.

But this was of short duration; for Absalom and his forces ere long appeared in sight, and David saw that a battle with his beloved son was inevitable. His forces had increased to many thousands, and, as with a heavy heart he drew them out, and placed them under his three captains, he commanded each to deal gently with the young man Absalom, for his sake; then retiring to his quarters, he undoubtedly prostrated himself before the Lord, to pray for his unnatural and cruel son. Meanwhile the battle was in progress, and Absalom, while riding furiously in his zeal to defeat his father, was caught by his long hair in a low branch of an oak, and there hung, the mule passing on from under him. Solomon never saw this brother again, and perhaps his last view of him was when

24   THE HISTORY OF KING SOLOMON.

he rode through the streets of Jerusalem in such pomp, exciting the envy of some and the admiration of others; but it was all past now, and Absalom lay a mangled corpse under a pile of stones in the land of Gilead.

Solomon gladly returned to Jerusalem with his parents, and entered once more his beloved home. But the death of Absalom had cast a dark shadow over the once happy palace, and a deep sorrow upon the hearts of the whole family. The revolt had also left the country in a very disturbed state, and jealousies and petty rebellions, springing up here and there, caused the king much trouble and perplexity.

All this, however, did not teach him wholly to obey the Lord; and when, some time after, he saw how greatly the country had extended and prospered under his reign, he began to cherish a wish to know just how many subjects he had capable of bearing arms. God had expressly forbidden his numbering the people, for the Lord could conquer by few as well as by many, and He was their Captain. Yet Joab was called, and ordered to go from one end of the land to the other, and bring in the number of the people. To this he made strong objections; but the king insisted, and Joab and his officers went forth. Nearly ten months were occupied in the accomplishment of this work, when he returned and reported one million and three hundred thousand valiant men who drew the bow.

Solomon was now old enough to see and realize in some degree, the great responsibilities that would soon rest upon him as the head of this vast army, for he probably knew that he was to succeed his father in the kingdom; but if he began to indulge in any flattering anticipations of his future greatness, they were speedily checked by the great perplexity and distress into which his father was thrown by a visit from the old prophet Gad. This prophet had been a firm friend of David's through all his former trials, while Saul was hunting him from one end of the land to the other, and had even been over into Moab with him during his exile: now he appears again, with a message from the Lord.

He assured the king that one of three great evils must come upon the land for his sin in numbering the people. "Shall seven years of famine come unto thee into thy land," said Gad; "or wilt thou flee three months before thy enemies, while they pursue thee; or that there be three days' pestilence? Now, advise and see what answer I shall return to Him that sent me."

David had been praying over his sin during the night, and had humbly repented of it; and now he was in a great strait, for it was hard to choose between these three great evils. At length, with an aching heart, he threw himself upon the mercies of the Lord, and left the disposal of the matter wholly with him. Then God sent forth the angel of death, and in three days seventy thousand of those over whom David had gloried, lay in their graves. In this was a lesson of wisdom for Solomon, which we trust he was not slow in learning. It was not far from this time probably, that he married Naamah, an Ammonitess, who was probably a proselyte to the true religion.

CHAPTER III.

Adonijah's Revolt—Solomon Crowned.

David, under the burden of his arduous duties and severe trials, was becoming prematurely old. Adonijah noticed this, and although he knew that Solomon had been appointed by God himself to sit upon the throne, he secretly determined to put in his claim as the eldest living son, and secure, if possible, the crown; so he kept a close lookout for a favorable opportunity in which to assert his claim. He was over thirty-three years of age at this time; and being very artful and sagacious, he succeeded in drawing Joab, his father's old and faithful general, into his plans, and also Abiathar one of the priests, and several other influential men; for he, like Absalom, had prepared himself royal chariots and many attendants.

Going down to En-rogel, a place a little out of Jerusalem, he made a magnificent feast, to which he invited all his brothers except Solomon, and all the principal men of Judah; and there they proclaimed Adonijah king, and had a general time of rejoicing. Nathan, the old prophet who thought much more of David and Solomon than he did of Adonijah the usurper, heard what was being done at En-rogel, and hastened in to tell Bathsheba. She was surprised and alarmed at his words; and he advised her, if she wished to save her own and Solomon's life, to go immediately to David, tell him what had been done, and remind him of his promise to her, which was that Solomon should be the king

David had been sick, but when she came in and bowed before him, he received her kindly and asked her errand. She reminded him of his promise; and then informed him that Adonijah had already been proclaimed king, and that the eyes of all the people were turned to him to know whom he would choose to reign after him.

At that moment Nathan entered, and after bowing himself to the ground before the king, repeated in substance what Bathsheba had said, and added, that while the captains of the host, the sons of the king, and many others had been called to attend Adonijah's feast, himself, Zadok, Benaiah, and Solomon had not been invited; and inquired if the thing had been known and ordered by the king.

David decided at once what to do. He called for Bathsheba, who had retired when Nathan entered; and when she came and stood before him, he looked earnestly upon her, and said, "As the Lord liveth, that hath redeemed my soul out of all distress, even as I sware unto thee by the Lord God of Israel, saying, Assuredly Solomon thy son shall reign after me, and he shall sit upon my throne in my stead, even so will I assuredly do this day."

Bathsheba was greatly pleased, and bowed herself before the king and said: "Let my lord, King David, live for ever."

It is a happy thing for young men in any of the walks of life, to have wise and active mothers to espouse their cause, and by their counsels, efforts, and prayers, to help them reach and honorably fill the stations allotted them in life; but it is sad to know that there are many in this day who disregard such influences, and think it manly to break away from maternal counsels.

David having finished his message to Bathsheba, immediately sent for Zadok the priest, Nathan the prophet, and Benaiah the captain of his guard. This Benaiah was a very valiant man, who once killed a lion in a pit in time of snow, and afterwards a giant who had a sword and a spear, while he had nothing but a staff. These three trusty friends of David soon entered and stood before the king. David raising himself in bed, said, "Take with you my body-guard, and bring the mule which

I ride upon, and take Solomon down to the brook Gihon, and there anoint him, and blow a trumpet, and say, God save King Solomon! Then bring him back into the city and place him upon my throne, for he shall be king in my stead."

Solomon was about eighteen years of age, and was a modest, unassuming young man, who felt himself to be but a child; yet relying upon God for help, he gladly submitted to his father's directions, and prepared for his inauguration. Zadok took from the tabernacle a horn of oil which was very fragrant and costly, while the people carried their instruments of music; and when they reached Gihon they anointed Solomon and blew the trumpets, and they all cried with a mighty voice, "God save King Solomon," and all the musicians played upon their instruments, and the people rejoiced with so great a joy that the earth rung again.

Adonijah and his company were just completing their feast as the noise of the people reached their ears; and Joab, starting up in alarm, inquired for the cause of the great uproar in the city. No wonder that his guilty conscience was terrified; for being one of the conspirators, he had forfeited his office and head. At that moment, a young man, Jonathan son of the priest, was seen hurriedly approaching; and Adonijah, throwing open the door, said, "Come in, for thou art a valiant man, and bringest good tidings."

Jonathan replied: "David has made Solomon king; he has been anointed, and is now seated upon the throne, and all the people are rejoicing. David has also received the congratulations of the people, and blessed the Lord for giving him a son to sit on the throne while he is still alive."

Abiathar the priest heard the words of his son Jonathan, who had probably come on purpose to save his father's life, and was greatly alarmed, as were also all of the company; and every man fled from Adonijah, leaving him alone, to sustain his usurped authority as best he could. Thus friends often gather around those in prosperity, with the hope of receiving some favor; but in times of adversity they are nowhere to be found, and like Adonijah's friends, are ashamed to acknowledge even their acquaintance.

Terribly alarmed, Adonijah gave up all for lost,

fled into the city, entered the tabernacle, and caught hold of the horns of the altar; while Joab, who had been so bold and courageous before, now cowered down under his guilt, and lay in some secret place, fearing the wrath of his cousin Solomon. The city was in confusion, and many were running here and there in search of the conspirators, when Solomon heard that Adonijah was clinging to the horns of the altar, and begging for life. He immediately sent him word that if he would show himself a worthy man he would protect him, but if not he should die. Guilty, and trembling with fear, he was brought before King Solomon, who ordered him to go home to his own house on parole. He afterwards did wrong again, and was put to death.

We can see by Adonijah's course and fate, that there is nothing gained by appropriating to ourselves what of right belongs to others; and our best rule is, "always to do by others as we would have them do by us."

CHAPTER IV.

David assembles the People—Gives a Charge to Solomon.

David was now seventy years old. He had long been out of health, and feeling that his end was nigh, and desiring to set his affairs in order and prepare to depart, he sent for Solomon, who came and stood before him. David told him that he knew he was young to assume the responsible duties of the kingdom, but that he must be strong, and show himself a man in capacity and judgment.

"And, my son," he added, "it was in my mind to build a house for the Lord, but I was forbidden to do it, because I was a man of war; but God said to me, 'Behold, a son shall be born to thee, who shall be a man of rest, and I will give him rest from all his enemies round about, for his name shall be Solomon—peaceable. He shall build a house for my name, and he shall be my son, and I will be his father.' Now, my son, go on and build the house of the Lord thy God. And if you obey the Lord in all things, and walk humbly before him, he will give you wisdom, and you shall prosper in all that you do. In the midst of my wars, cares, and troubles, I have never lost sight of the temple, but have been laying aside what I could for that purpose. You will find ready one hundred thousand talents of gold, a thousand thousand talents of silver, and brass and iron without weight, for it is in abundance. As for timber and stone, I have prepared a great deal, but you can add to it as you need. Besides, you have masons and carpenters, and men who can do all manner of curious work, and the temple can be commenced without delay."

David had been a king nearly forty years, and

knew that his influence with the heads of the nation would be more than Solomon's could possibly be at that time; and to further the work which he had just given his son, he thought best to call together the principal men of the kingdom, lay the subject before them, and secure to Solomon their coöperation.

Messengers were accordingly despatched in every direction, and at the set time, there arrived at Jerusalem all the princes of Israel, the princes of the tribes, and the captains of the companies that ministered to the king by course, and the captains over the thousands, and the captains over the hundreds, and the stewards over the possessions of the king and his sons, with the officers and with the mighty men, and with all the valiant men. Here were the wisdom, valor, and power of the whole nation, standing before their aged and beloved king, to listen to a few parting words from him, in regard to the great interests of his country and his God.

With renewed strength given for this solemn occasion, David wrapped his garments about him, and stood upon his feet. Every eye of that vast assembly was fixed upon him in tender sympathy, as he said: "Hear me, my brethren, and my people." He then proceeded to tell them that at one time he had purposed to build a house to the Lord, and had made ready many materials, but God had ordered that it should be left for Solomon to accomplish. Then, after rehearsing many of God's dealings with them, he raised his hand and charged them in the sight of all Israel, the congregation of the Lord, and in the audience of God, to seek for and keep all the commandments of the Lord; that they might retain the good country in which they lived, and leave it for their children after them for ever.

David then turning to his son, said: "And thou, Solomon, my son, know thou the God of thy father, and serve him with a perfect heart and with a willing mind, for the Lord searcheth all hearts and understandeth all the imaginations of the thoughts: if thou seek him he will be found of thee, but if thou forsake him he will cast thee off for ever. Take heed now, for the Lord hath chosen thee to build a house for the sanctuary; be strong, and do it."

David then furnished Solomon with plans of the temple, both internal and external, which had been given him, he said, by the Spirit of God. Nothing had been left to the wisdom or discretion of Solomon, for even the weight of the gold for each instrument and vessel was given by his father. After this was completed, David, turning again to the people, told them that, besides the regular proportions of the spoils of his enemies which he invariably consecrated to the Lord, he had from his own private means given three thousand talents of pure gold—which, according to the estimate of some, amounts to over seventy-two millions of dollars. Besides this, he had given seven thousand talents of silver, or over ten and a half millions of dollars. And when he inquired who was willing to assist by contributing of his wealth for this service, every heart responded, and about one hundred and eighty millions more in gold and silver was offered, besides brass, precious stones, and iron. It was given willingly, and all rejoiced together. David remembered whence came all good gifts, and led the people in prayer and praise to the Lord God of Israel. He then called upon the congregation to bless the Lord, and they all bowed their heads and worshipped the Lord; after which they offered burnt-offerings, and dispersed for the night.

The next day this assembly came together again, and cattle, sheep, and lambs were driven in for offerings, till Jerusalem was full of their lowings and bleatings. Three thousand sinless creatures were laid upon the altar, and their blood poured out for the guilt of the nation, thus typifying that greater sacrifice which was yet to come. On the peace-offerings the people were allowed to feast, and they all ate and drank before the Lord, with great gladness.

Solomon had been hastily, and by a very few people, anointed king but a short time before; now it was proposed that the ceremony should be repeated before the princes and mighty men of the nation. So Solomon was again anointed, and amid the loud acclamations and rejoicings of the people, he was taken back to the palace and placed upon the throne of his father. Never before had Palestine witnessed such triumphal proceedings, for neither Saul nor David had been as highly exalted in the eyes of the nation as this young man Solomon. At length the congregation broke up and returned to their homes, rejoicing in the royal majesty of their new sovereign.

David came from obscurity and poverty, but his course was uniformly onward and upward, and the hope which he anchored in God stood sure and steadfast to the end. Solomon, on the contrary, flashes upon our vision like a burning meteor, and promises a career which shall eclipse every thing which had gone before.

His first duty seems to have been to bury his father, who died soon after he relinquished the throne. He left great riches, and a conquered territory extending from the river Euphrates on the east, to the river of Egypt on the southwest; but his best bequest was a united kingdom, and a loving and loyal people.

In the first year of Solomon's reign, his heart was gladdened by the birth of a son, an heir to the crown, whom he named Rehoboam. The event awakened new feelings, and stirred for the first time, the deep fountains of parental love in the heart of the young king; but the child was laid in the arms of Naamah its mother, while Solomon attended to the weighty matters of the kingdom.

The fame of the Israelites had spread into distant lands, and Pharaoh, king of Egypt, made an alliance with Solomon, that their mutual interests might the better be promoted; and as another proof of his regard, he gave him his daughter for a wife, and she was brought in pomp and splendor from her father's heathen court, to Jerusalem. There she was to live till Solomon should finish the temple, when he designed to build a house expressly for her, for he said: "My wife shall not dwell in the house of David, king of Israel, because the places are holy whereunto the ark of the Lord hath come." She was of heathen extraction, and even if proselyted, she was probably surrounded by many heathen attendants, whose practices would profane a sacred place.

Solomon was as yet disposed to obey the injunctions of his father, and observe the worship which he had been taught from a child to respect; and he is said to have loved the Lord, yet he allowed idolatrous worship on many a hill in his kingdom.

Added to this, he had one heathen wife, and probably more, who had views of their own in regard to worship; and Solomon had, in thus marrying, both placed himself in the way of temptation, and openly broken one of the commands of God. Some have believed that these wives were proselyted to the Jewish faith, but for this opinion there is no evidence; and it would not have been strange if the little boy Rehoboam had grown up an idolater, and become a wicked king.

CHAPTER V.

Solomon at Gibeon—His Wise Choice—He judges between the Two Mothers.

It will be remembered that the tabernacle made in the time of Moses, and the brazen altar attached to it, were not in Jerusalem, but at Gibeon, a city about six miles north. There the priests of the Lord performed their duties according to the law, and there Solomon proposed to offer a solemn sacrifice in honor of God. Following the example of his father, he called for all the great men of the nation; and when they arrived, having procured a thousand animals for burnt-offerings, they all proceeded to Gibeon.

This place had belonged to the Hivites, but was captured by Joshua, which caused much consternation at the time throughout that region; and its inhabitants are the same who took mouldy bread, and clothed themselves in old garments and shoes, and came to Joshua, and through deceptive words induced him to enter into a league with them, and to make the promise to leave them in the quiet possession of their city for ever. But in after years, king Saul, in his zeal to exterminate the ancient inhabitants, broke the compact, and attempted to expel them from the country, for which sin God sent a famine upon the land in the time of David. See 2 Samuel 21. But notwithstanding these troubles, the tabernacle was located there, and Solomon and all the congregation with him went up to the altar, and offered upon it a thousand burnt-offerings. How long it took to do this we are not told; but at night, weary with the fatigue and excitement of the day, Solomon retired to rest. His bodily senses were soon locked in sleep; but while he slept his mind was supernatu-

SOLOMON AT GIBEON.

rally aroused—God appeared to him in a vision, and said: "Ask what I shall give thee."

Solomon manifested no fear on being thus addressed by the great Jehovah; but following the reflections which probably passed daily through his mind, he replied that God had showed great kindness to David his father and prospered him according as he had walked in his integrity, and had now bestowed upon himself the kingdom, instead of giving it to Adonijah, his elder brother. "And now, O Lord," he said, "I am but a little child; I know not how to go out or come in, and I am in the midst of thy people which thou hast chosen—a great people that cannot be numbered, nor counted for multitude. Give, therefore, thy servant an understanding heart to judge thy people, that I may discern between good and bad; for who is able to judge this thy so great a people?"

The wisdom of Solomon is discernible in this answer, and is worthy of the imitation of young men in every age of the world. God was pleased with his choice, and granted his request, assuring him that his wisdom should excel the wisdom of all the kings who had gone before or should come after him. And moreover, he should have that for which he had not asked, both riches and honor. Then came a conditional promise of long life, in case he was as devoted and obedient as his father.

SOLOMON AT GIBEON.

In the morning Solomon awoke and found that these revelations had been made in a dream; but they were real to him, and he went forth to his duties comforted and strengthened. Solomon and the people returned to Jerusalem, and stood before the ark of the covenant of the Lord, which was kept under a tent, and there they offered burnt-offerings and peace-offerings. It was proper that in presenting their sin-offerings at Gibeon, the people should fast and humble themselves before the Lord; but at Jerusalem they came with peace-offerings before a reconciled God, and rejoiced in his mercy, and they all ate of the peace-offerings, which furnished a feast to the whole people. The days of worship were ended, a great blessing had been secured to Solomon, and all the princes and great men of the nation took their leave of the king and returned to their homes.

After this, Solomon was seated upon his throne one day, to hear the causes of those who should come with complaints, when two women were admitted into his presence, each carrying a little babe in her arms. As they came near, Solomon saw that one of the children was dead. The woman carrying it bowed before him, and in great excitement, said: "Oh, my lord, this dead child belongs to that woman, and the living child is mine; she stole it from my bed, and put this one in its place while I was asleep." "No," interrupted the other; "the living child is mine, and the dead one yours." The first speaker was equally vehement in affirming what she had first said, while her opponent, clinging to the living child, persisted in saying that it was her own.

Solomon had probably never seen these women before, and how should he be expected to give a just decision in the case? One thing he did know, which was, that mothers loved their children dearly, and would suffer any thing themselves rather than have them harmed; and to test this feeling in the women before him, he proposed to cut the living babe in two, and give each a part. A sword was ordered, and when it was brought, Solomon said: "Cut the child in two, and divide it between them."

Horror-stricken at these words, the mother cried, "Oh, my lord, do not kill it; but let her keep it, let her keep it."

The other, with cold indifference, handing the child towards the executioner, answered: "Let it be neither mine nor thine; divide it."

Solomon had very adroitly arrived at the truth, and giving the child to its mother, sent them away.

The people throughout the country were greatly astonished at the wisdom of their young king, and they feared him because they saw that the wisdom of God was with him.

Solomon now began to execute his plans in regard to the temple; and as Hiram, king of Tyre had sent messengers to Jerusalem, to condole with him on account of the death of his father, he thought best to send a delegation back with them, to ask of Hiram the services of some of his master-workmen.

Hiram, on the reception of this word, was greatly pleased to learn that Solomon was disposed to carry out the wishes of his father, and returned answer that his workmen were at his disposal, and that he would order them to prepare cedar and fir-trees up in the mountain, get them down to the sea, and there make them into rafts or floats, to be sent wherever he should direct. This was very kind in Hiram, but no more so than Solomon had reason to expect, for he had been a firm friend of David's for years; and many suppose that he was a convert to the Jewish faith.

Solomon immediately made a levy upon the people, and raised thirty thousand men, ten thousand of whom were to be sent every month to Lebanon, to assist in the labor there. He had spoken freely to Hiram in praise of his own God, lest perhaps this king over an idolatrous nation, should receive the impression that a house, however large and magnificent, could contain the God he worshipped. "The temple," he said, "was designed merely as a place in which to burn sacrifices to the God whom the heaven of heavens could not contain, for he was above all gods."

There were men in the kingdom who worked skilfully in gold and silver; but Solomon wanted a head workman to direct all the rest, and he requested Hiram to send a man who was qualified to fill such a post, and could work exquisitely in gold, silver, brass, iron, purple, crimson, and blue. For such and other labor, Solomon was to pay yearly, twenty thousand measures of wheat, the same of barley, and twenty thousand baths of oil, and twenty thousand of wine, amounting to nearly five thousand barrels of each. As fast as the timber was prepared, it was floated down to Joppa, the nearest seaport, whence it was taken to Jerusalem.

While these preparations were going forward in Mount Lebanon, Solomon ordered great and costly hewed stones to be brought, to lay the foundation of the house. Josephus says: "they were cut and fitted together in the mountain, and then brought to the city, where they were laid very deep in the earth, that they might be able to bear the superstructure that was to be raised over them."

Within a few years, men of science have succeeded in entering the Turkish mosque of Omar, which now stands upon the spot once occupied by the temple; and in exploring its deep foundations, find stones of immense size, which are believed to be the same placed there so long ago by Solomon. But whether the dark, subterraneous passages which have recently been discovered, leading from the temple to the outer walls of the city, were made at that time, we do not know. Several such underground channels cut in solid rock, have recently been discovered, with the chips of the quarrying still lying in the sides of the passage.

Dr. Bement, who has travelled extensively in Egypt and Palestine, states, "that a German has recently explored one of these passages, and found that it had many branches, leading to several spacious apartments in which were many relics; among others were seen the bones of a camel. There can be little doubt that these passages were known to

Solomon, if indeed he did not himself order their construction."

Three years were occupied in making preparations for the temple, but in the fourth of Solomon's reign, the foundations were laid.

Apart from its courts, it was but a small structure, being about one hundred and five feet long, thirty wide, and forty-five high. It faced the east,

SOLOMON AT GIBEON. 59

and on that end had a porch or ornamental steeple one hundred and eighty feet high, overlaid within with pure gold. The entire body of the house up to the roof was made of white stone, which was fitted at the quarry, so that there was neither hammer, nor axe, nor any tool of iron heard in the house while it was in building.

Having finished the main part, he proceeded to overlay the ceilings and the doors, the posts and the walls with pure gold, garnishing with precious stones for beauty.

One room, called the "Holy of Holies," was thirty feet square, and overlaid with pure gold. Here the high-priest was admitted to God's presence once a year, on the great day of atonement; but no other person was ever allowed to enter within its hallowed walls. There was to be the ark, and there, with outstretched wings, reaching from ceiling to ceiling, stood two cherubim looking down upon the mercy-seat. These, and all other things in that room were covered with pure gold, which must have been worth several millions of dollars. A splendid veil hung at the entrance, made of blue and crimson. and fine linen, with figures of cherubim inwrought. At the death of Christ, the veil before the Most Holy place was rent in two, thus showing that the mercy-seat henceforth should be accessible to all.

The temple, when finished, was the most splendid and magnificent structure the world ever saw, and was typical of that house not made with hands, where the righteous will reign for ever with the Lord.

CHAPTER VI.

THE DEDICATION—SOLOMON'S PALACE.

NEARLY a year passed by after the completion of the temple, before the people were called together to its dedication. Then the call was given, and all the great men of

62   THE HISTORY OF KING SOLOMON.

the nation, besides an innumerable company of others, assembled at Jerusalem. It was on the eighth day of the seventh month, corresponding nearly to our October, that the ceremonies began. The king, attired in his royal robes, and surrounded by all

his principal officers and the priests, proceeded with the multitude to that part of the city where the ark of the Lord had been kept, and there they offered up sacrifices, sheep and oxen, in great numbers. The priests and Levites then took up the ark, and amid music and rejoicings carried it to the temple, and placed it in the Holy of Holies, under the spread wings of the golden cherubim.

Several thousand singers, dressed in white linen robes, were gathered near the altar, with cymbals, harps, and psalteries in their hands, while a hundred and twenty priests with trumpets stood near; and at a given signal every instrument and voice sounded in harmonious concert, praising the Lord for his goodness and his mercy, which endureth for ever.

Suddenly the whole house was filled with a cloud, so that the priests could not stand to minister before the altar; and as it gathered over the congregation, Solomon worshipped and praised the Lord, and blessed the people in His name. Then kneeling before the altar, he addressed the Lord in a long, humble, and earnest prayer. As he finished, fire from heaven came down upon the animals that were bleeding upon the altar, and consumed them; and the glory of the Lord filled the house, and all the people bowed their faces to the pavement, and worshipped and praised the Lord.

During this solemn dedication and festival which continued two weeks, Solomon offered twenty-two thousand oxen, and a hundred and twenty thousand sheep. Upon these the whole people feasted, while they rejoiced greatly in the piety, wisdom, and liberality of their young king. At the termination of the solemnities, Solomon blessed all the congregation with a loud voice, and sent them away in peace.

He was deeply interested in what had been transpiring; and as he lay asleep in the night, God appeared to him as he had before done at Gibeon, and assured him that He had heard his prayer, and had hallowed the house which he had built for his worship. He also promised Solomon, in case he was faithful to obey him in all things, to continue the kingdom to him and his children for ever; but

THE DEDICATION.

if he or they should turn aside to worship other gods, they should be driven from the land, and the beautiful temple so spoiled, that every one who saw it should be astonished, and hiss. Solomon and his son did not fully obey the Lord, and only thirty-three years after this, the temple was plundered by Shishak, king of Egypt. It subsequently suffered various profanations, and about four hundred and twenty-four years after its erection, it was entirely destroyed by Nebuchadnezzar.

Solomon probably felt as many other young men have, while not guilty of great crimes, that he was capable of self-control, and though he should put himself in the way of temptation by marrying heathen wives, he should not be led into idolatry by their example. We never know our own strength in resisting evil till it is tried, therefore we should daily pray, "Lead us not into temptation."

The first eleven years of Solomon's reign went by prosperously. The house of the Lord was finished, and every morning and evening, without intermission, according to the command of the Lord, an innocent lamb was offered, which typified " the Lamb of God which taketh away the sin of the world." This ceremony Solomon was careful to maintain, for upon it rested a promise, and he was anxious to retain God as his friend. He had now become a great monarch; he was leagued with Hiram, king of Tyre; Pharaoh was his father-in-law, and his dominions stretched from the Mediterranean to the Euphrates, and from far north of Damascus down to the river of Egypt. Moreover, the fame of his greatness and wisdom had spread throughout all the nations around him, and princes and great men with presents of great value, were continually coming to Jerusalem to witness his unequalled splendor. The house of cedar which David had built with Hiram's assistance, and in which Solomon had been brought up, was not now suited to his wants, and he laid the foundations of one of

THE DEDICATION.

the most magnificent palaces of his day. Josephus informs us that "it was a large and curious building, made entirely of white stone, cedar-wood, gold and silver."

Palaces in those days occupied in some instances several acres of ground, which were enclosed with high and strong walls. Within these were buildings of every description, for the entertainment of thousands of guests; while groves, fountains, and gardens beautified the place. Most buildings had open courts in the centre, with galleries encircling three sides, supported by large marble pillars. The building which Solomon erected for his palace was one hundred and fifty-five feet long, seventy-five wide and forty-five high, the pillars being of cedar, in quadrangular form. There was also another structure over against the palace, raised upon massive pillars, with a court attached, in which was a splendid room where Solomon sat to judge the people. To this was joined a palace for the queen, and in other localities were smaller edifices for his vast household. A large number of great and costly stones were cut from the quarry with saws, and after they had been carved in a very curious manner, with representations of trees and plants with pendant leaves, they were placed in the house for walls and ceilings. The carving is said to have completely covered the stone, and the leaves were made so thin and natural that a person would almost expect to see them stirred by the air.

Several other edifices are mentioned by Josephus, and among them a splendid room for feasting, where all the dishes were of pure gold. "Now it is very hard," he adds, "to reckon up the variety and magnitude of the royal apartments, how many that were subterraneous and invisible; the curious form of those that enjoyed the fresh air; and the groves, for the most delightful prospect and the avoiding of the heat."

THE DEDICATION. 69

Solomon also built a great throne of ivory, overlaid with the purest gold. On either side of the seat, as he sat before the people, stood two lions; and on the six steps by which he ascended the throne stood twelve lions, six on the one side and six on the other; there was not the like made in any kingdom. This structure was thirteen years in building, and some idea can be formed of the spacious palace and its occupants, when we remember that "there was supplied every day for those who fed at the king's table, two hundred and eighty bushels of fine flour, five hundred and sixty bushels of meal, ten fat oxen, and twenty oxen out of the pastures, and a hundred sheep, besides harts and roebucks, and fallow deer, and fatted fowl." Twelve officers were appointed to make provision for the king's table, each acting one month out of the twelve.

We of this nineteenth century, with our new inventions and boasted improvements, are apt to think that we are emphatically *the* people, and that the ancients were comparatively an inferior race; but where can we now look for such skilful workmanship, such affluence and gorgeous display, united with unequalled wisdom, as in the reign of Solomon, who lived nearly three thousand years ago? During the first twenty-four years of his reign, he accomplished more in elevating and enriching the nation, than had ever before been effected.

Under the Phœnicians, the Israelites had been taking lessons in the arts of building, farming, quarrying, and navigation; arts in which they had hitherto been very deficient.

But prosperity is not generally favorable to a spirit of piety, and Solomon was daily becoming more and more absorbed in the affairs of the world, and less sensitive to the wickedness which met him on every hand. Idolatry was insinuating itself into the very heart of the nation, and even Solomon himself was doing more for its establishment, than

THE DEDICATION.

any other individual in the kingdom. For, very frequently, some young and beautiful heathen princess, with all her love for idol worship, was transplanted, contrary to the express command of God, from her own native home to the palace of Solomon, where she exerted over him and others her baneful influence.

Among these was a woman from Sidon, a city in Phœnicia. This country, so famed in history, was only about one hundred and twenty miles long, and twenty broad, but it had five cities of note. Arad was in the extreme north; eighteen miles south lay, and still lies, Tripolis; still farther south was Berytus, now Beyroot, which in 1823 became a missionary station, where the Rev. Dr. Eli Smith and others have labored with much success. The next city south was Sidon, supposed to have been built by the eldest son of Canaan, which would give it an age of at least a thousand years before Solomon. Then came Tyre, Hiram's capital, which was of great renown, having colonies and ports of its own on many other shores. Carthage, that old and illustrious city on the African coast, was their colony, and on the southwestern coast of Spain was a port of theirs, called Tarshish, or Tartessus. Ships bound to that port often made long and adventurous voyages, and on that account were called "ships of Tarshish." On one of these Jonah took passage, when fleeing from the Lord.

The Tyrians also had ports in the Persian Gulf, from which they received many goods. Being skilled in ship-building, they excelled all other nations of that day in the art of navigation. Their ship boards were made from fir-trees, their masts of cedar, and their oars of the oaks of Bashan. Their benches were partly of ivory, and their sails were fine embroidered linen from Egypt. With pilots from Sidon, their old capitol, they sailed into different countries, and traded extensively in all kinds of riches—gold, silver, tin, lead, brass, and horses, fine linen, coral, and agate. And it is said that they even sailed around the southern cape of Africa, where "they were brought into great waters, and were broken by the sea." They visited the Ionian islands and Greece, where they purchased cassia, calamus, and other products of the country. They also bought the persons of men from foreigners, and chests of rich apparel, and precious cloths for chariots. See Ezekiel, chap. 27.

Thus Tyre was flourishing when Solomon made a league with Hiram, and married, it is said, his daughter. Phœnicia was more enlightened in regard to literature, than any other nation then in existence, and had in the time of Joshua sent letters and science by Cadmus into Greece.

In order to gratify this Sidonian lady whom he had married, Solomon built a temple to Astoreth, one of her gods, on the Mount of Olives, in view of the temple of his own God; and not many years passed before, for similar reasons, a temple was erected to Chemosh, the god of the Moabites. His Ammonitess wife then preferred her claim, and Solomon granted her request, and built a temple for Moloch, or Milcom, near the same spot. The worshippers of this cruel god, supposing that he could be pleased by the screams and cries of tormented children, compelled their little ones to pass through the fire, or cast them into the red-hot arms of his image, while with drums, the people drowned their agonies. These sounds must have mingled very discordantly with the solemn worship in Jehovah's temple; and it is surprising that Solomon, with all his wisdom, could tolerate practices so revolting and inhuman, and in the eyes of his own God, so dreadfully wicked. But we must remember that many steps in his downward course had been taken before he openly sanctioned these abominations. His first sin lay in placing himself in the way of temptation by marrying heathen wives, after which there was no security for him, and he ran

THE DEDICATION. 75

his downward course with rapidity. The worship at the temple Chemosh is supposed to have consisted " in revelling and drunkenness, obscenities and impurities of the grossest kind ;" and Solomon may have satisfied his conscience with the idea that he was in circumstances which he could not control, and that, as a good and kind husband, he must wink at some practices which his heart condemned.

The king had become a great architect; and as he never did any thing on a small scale, all these palaces and temples were no doubt made after his own ideas of splendor and magnificence. During all this building, Solomon called freely upon Hiram, king of Tyre, for wood, stone, gold, and workmen, and consequently, a national debt had been created of considerable magnitude, which Solomon wished to cancel. Having twenty cities lying on the north of Palestine, which are supposed to have been captured from the neighboring province, Solomon offered them to Hiram, who seemed to think them a sufficient remuneration. Some time after, however, he took a journey over that part of the country to see them, and as he went from one to another, he found them either in ruins, or of so little worth, that he returned home quite displeased, and sent word to Solomon that they were not such cities as he wanted. Hiram called them the land of Cabul, or that which displeases. Solomon probably found means to satisfy the claims of Hiram, for these two kings continued friends, and assisted each other for many years after. The twenty cities in question Solomon afterwards repaired, and retained in his own kingdom.

Not far from this time, Pharaoh, king of Egypt, seems to have visited his daughter; and as she was settled so magnificently in her own house, she probably entertained him and his courtiers in great pomp. Why he came into Palestine is not stated, but as he was Solomon's ally, as well as father-in-law, it is not at all surprising that he should visit

THE DEDICATION. 77

the country. He may have been out on a campaign, and merely called on his return, for we read of his doing nothing in that neighborhood, except conquering Gezer, a city of the Canaanites, between Jerusalem and the Mediterranean, which he gave to his daughter. This city had been left, by Joshua and the judges, to its old heathen inhabitants, who paid tribute to Israel; but this Egyptian king appears to have destroyed or expelled all the remaining Canaanites in it, for the sake of giving his daughter a present. It is to be hoped that he returned home without further slaughter or conquests. Soon after, Solomon sent out his men, and rebuilt and walled his wife's city, for it was a place naturally strong, and might be of service to the country in time of war. The two Beth-horons, Upper and Lower, which lay about twelve miles northwest of Jerusalem, needed repairing, and Solomon's men were ordered to go to work upon them, which they did. Large and strong walls, with heavy gates and bars, were built, and the whole was finished according to the king's direction.

Notwithstanding Solomon had so much to do, and so much to do with, he frequently returned to his great and splendid palace, feeling as many men in poorer circumstances have since done, "that all was vanity and vexation of spirit." There is one thing which the readers of this little book may not yet understand, and would not perhaps believe if they were told it; which is, that there is nothing in this world's riches that can make them perfectly happy. If you live to realize all your present anticipations, you will feel at last, like Solomon, that you need something else to make you truly blessed.

CHAPTER VII.

Solomon's Spirit of Enterprise—His Experiments.

Far at the east of Palestine lay the Babylonian empire, with its great rivers Euphrates and Tigris, and their tributaries, watering thousands of acres of rich and cultivated land, while numberless cities teeming with human beings, lay in the plains between, or on the shores of the gulf, and in the vast region beyond. To secure an exchange of products with these people was an object of great interest with western nations.

Large caravans, loaded with eastern wealth, were frequently arriving at the cities of Phœnicia, or passing on to the western country of Asia-Minor. Solomon saw the golden stream, and determined to turn it into his own reservoirs. Damascus, that great emporium of trade, was already in his possession, it having been conquered in the time of David, his father; and in order to facilitate travel with the interior, it was deemed necessary to build a city in the great valley between Mount Lebanon, Phœnicia's western boundary, and Anti-Lebanon, which lay farther at the east. There are at this day extensive ruins of a city lying in this locality, called Baalbeck, which is supposed by many to have been the same that Solomon built at that time. Very little is said in the Bible concerning this city, but some things in the style of architecture go to show that Solomon was its builder. On the pillars and their caps, and upon the lintels of the doors of a heathen temple in the city, are found the carved lily, the emblem of peace, whose leaves are often from twelve to eighteen inches in length; the pomegranate, signifying plenty, and the net-work, typical of unity or brotherly love; and

SOLOMON'S SPIRIT OF ENTERPRISE.

a late writer observes: "There is now no room to doubt that this temple was erected by Solomon, and that Baalbeck is the Baalath of the Bible."

This was not the first temple of the kind to which he had given his influence and money. The ruins at Baalbeck surpass in magnificence almost all the ancient ruins that have been found.

An Arabian writer says: "Baalbeck is a city of three' days journey west of Damascus, where are wonderful structures and magnificent vestiges of antiquity, and palaces with marble columns, such as in the whole world are nowhere else to be found." The temple, according to Dr. Bement's measurement, is eight hundred feet long and five hundred feet wide, and would accommodate many thousands of worshippers. Part of the wall of the temple is composed of blocks of hard sandstone, so perfectly polished and adjusted to each other, that it would be difficult to insert a fine knife-blade between them. Three of the stones in the wall surrounding the city, are severally ten feet through, fourteen feet high, and sixty-eight long; and by what mighty power these were placed in their present position, is a mystery to the wisest architects of the present day. It was a great achievement, and Solomon no doubt was elated with the wonderful works which he had accomplished, when he exclaimed: "Lo, I am come to great estate, and have gotten more wisdom than all they who have gone before me in Jerusalem."

Flattering rumors also of his wisdom had gone through the then known world, and perhaps his self-complacency was not a little increased, as day after day courtiers and princes from foreign countries arrived, to seek his favor and pay him honor. It is quite natural that the human heart, under such circumstances, should be inflated with pride; but in the retiracy of his own chamber, Solomon took rational views of life, and saw that nothing could be enjoyed in this world, which would fully satisfy the human soul.

Determining, however, to leave nothing untried in the pursuit of pleasure, and possessing some of the musical taste of his father, he provided his luxurious palace with a select band of musicians, both male and female, and supplied them with all kinds of musical instruments. The numerous ladies and children of the palace were no doubt greatly delighted with this arrangement, and Solomon himself may have thought that he had in a great measure secured the happiness for which he sought. He also for a time gave himself up to mirth, and was surrounded by the most witty, gay, and dissipated of his courtiers, to see if there was any real good or happiness in that course of life. Many seemed to enjoy with a keen relish the jolly humor which he was testing; but Solomon, after a fair trial, declared that laughter was madness, and that mirth added nothing to substantial pleasure.

Observing that wine elated the spirits of its admirers, he concluded to give that a fair test, and indulge his appetite, and see what it could do for him; yet he determined to conduct the experiment with wisdom, and not give himself up to excess. It was a dangerous experiment even for this wise man; and it is surely great folly for any one with less wisdom to tamper with so dangerous a foe. He saw that this too was all folly; and although for the moment cares might be forgotten and trials lightened, yet in the end sorrow and disgust were the consequence.

These courses and all similar ones he then left for the foolish; while he attempted to satisfy himself in the more rational way of improving his own premises and estates. He planted vineyards and beautiful gardens, and at a very great expense made orchards and parks, transplanting trees in them of all kinds of fruit, both of such as were natural to that climate, and also those which were brought from other countries; and lest they should die in droughts, he made great pools for water at vast expense, and by some contrivance succeeded in conveying this water to his gardens and orchards. Three very large reservoirs near Bethlehem, the water of which is conveyed to Jerusalem in an ancient aqueduct, are still called Solomon's Pools. This was a pleasant employment, and served to amuse and divert him for some time. He also had numerous servants, ready to go at his bidding; and as for cattle, no one who had ever lived in Jerusalem had as many or as great a variety. The same might be said in regard to his wives; for they, like the trees of his gardens, were gathered from all countries, and transplanted with all their foreign customs into that land of promise, and needed constant watching and training to get and keep them in the right way. But as there were seven hundred or a thousand of them, it was too much for any one man to attempt, and Solomon was obliged to yield in a great measure to this foreign influence, and found himself at length very far from the principles he had formed in his youth. The marrying of so many heathen wives was the most sinful and pernicious of all his experiments after happiness.

Taking a retrospective view of his course in life to secure pleasure, he declared that the whole was vanity and vexation of spirit, without the least real profit; and his testimony on this subject ought surely to be believed, for his opportunities for judging were better than those of any other man. Yet the young are incredulous, and each person prefers to try the foolish experiment of pleasure-seeking for himself.

Solomon's prosperity was constantly on the increase, and the whole nation over whom he ruled looked upon him with reverence and gratification, and probably concluded that their wisdom in choosing a king was not to be questioned, whatever might have been thought of it years before by the old prophet Samuel. But the outward prosperity of a nation is not always a sure index to their real condition; as we see in the case of the Israelites, who were so infatuated by the wealth and flattery that poured in upon them from every quarter, that they failed to observe the canker-sore of idolatry, which was eating out their very existence. It is true, an outward show of religion was kept up at the temple, and that every evening and morning a lamb without spot or blemish was laid upon the altar as an atonement for sin, which served to keep in remembrance that greater Sacrifice which was to come, and towards which this pointed; for without the shedding of blood, there is no remission of sins.

As long as this worship was observed, God promised to meet with and bless his people; so Christians in all ages may hope for similar blessings, if they, through the blood of Christ, hold communion daily with an offended but merciful God.

CHAPTER VIII.

THE GOLDEN SHIELDS—TADMOR OF THE WILDERNESS—SHIP-BUILDING.

Solomon, having a large amount of gold, which had been accumulating from different sources, and no war occurring to call for its use, employed skilful workmen and made up some of it into shields, which were designed probably for his body-guard on great occasions. Two hundred of these shields were of superior worth, while three hundred were of less weight; but they were all of pure gold, and are estimated to have been worth over a million of dollars. A vast amount of money, truly, to be expended on articles for mere pomp and display, and to hang idly upon the walls of the house of Lebanon, where these were placed when out of

THE GOLDEN SHIELDS.

use. Admiring visitors, it is true, beheld in wonder this display of the wealth of the sovereign, but there were better uses for riches then, as now: were this amount now placed in the treasury of the Lord, and used to scatter the glad news of salvation, angels would rejoice over returning and repenting sinners, who would behold with wonder the boundless wealth of mercy there is in the King of kings.

Solomon also prepared himself one thousand and four hundred chariots, and twelve thousand horsemen. Forty thousand stalls for horses were made in the different cities of his kingdom, and these cities were put in a state of complete defence, and stored with corn, wine, and oil; and had a war occurred, they would have been places of safety, into which the people could have run for protection. But for years no enemy appeared, and the country increased in wealth and enterprise.

Solomon saw that the walls which surrounded

the city of Jerusalem were not sufficiently strong to keep out an invading army, and ordered his engineers to go to work and strengthen them, and to place towers upon the top, where men in time of battle could shelter themselves while they fought their foes. The city was strongly fortified by nature, for on three sides were deep valleys; but, besides this, strong walls extended all around the city.

These works being accomplished, Solomon's attention was turned to the difficulties which travellers to the East had to encounter in crossing that long, bleak desert, into which they at once struck on leaving Damascus. Every now and then a fierce hot wind from the south set in motion the burning sand, and greatly endangered the lives of travellers. For three days' journey, no tree, nor stream of water, nor shrub, nor grass, nor verdure of any kind was to be seen; and a bed in the sand was the only lodging-place on this route. There were a few verdant spots on the desert, and after about a hundred miles of travel from Damascus, one of some size met the longing gaze of the weary travellers, where a few palm-trees grew luxuriantly near a fountain of water. Every heart revived at this sight, and even the patient camels quickened their pace to reach a spot where their thirst might be quenched; but ferocious beasts of prey lurked here in ambush, which greatly endangered the safety and comfort of the travellers. Great and almost insurmountable difficulties must be encountered in attempting to build a city in such a place, for there was neither wood nor stone to be had upon the oasis. Yet with characteristic perseverance, Solomon determined to do it, and ordered his men to commence the work. How long the city was in building we are not told, but a modern traveller who visited "Tadmor of the wilderness," describes its ruins as extensive and grand. The remains of a large temple with its ornamented carvings of the lily, the pomegranate and net-work, plainly point back to the days of Solomon. Some of the stones in the walls are immense, similar in size to those at Baalbec; yet there are no quarries where they could have been dug nearer than one hundred miles across the desert; and by what power they were transported that distance, remains as yet an impenetrable mystery. Palaces and dwellings, however, came into existence, and there in the heart of the desert sprung up the city of Tadmor or Palmyra, with its thousands of human beings, eager in the chase of life.

Josephus, in speaking of it, says, "Solomon went as far as the desert above Syria, and possessed himself of it, and built there a very great city, which was distant two days' journey from Upper Syria, and one day's journey from the Euphrates, and six days' journey from Babylon the great. Now the reason why this city lay so remote from the parts of Syria that are inhabited, is this: that below, there is no water to be had, and it is in that place only that there are springs and pits of water. When he had therefore built this city and encompassed it with very strong walls, he gave it the name of Tadmor, but the Greeks called it Palmyra." By the protection of this city the perils of the desert-trade, though still terrible, were greatly mitigated; for there caravans found rest, food, and shelter.

Wealth, now, through Tadmor, Damascus, and Baalbec, and from various other sources, poured in upon Solomon, till he surpassed all the kings of the earth in his riches, while his wisdom was unparalleled. As a scholar and writer in the sciences and literature of his day he was unequalled: he composed a thousand and five songs, and three thousand proverbs, of which those that have been preserved are worthy of the careful study and attention of the young in every age. "He spake of trees, from the cedar-tree that is in Lebanon, even unto the hyssop that springeth out of the wall;

he spake also of beasts, and of fowl, and of creeping things, and of fishes." "And all the kings of the earth sought the presence of Solomon, to hear his wisdom that God had put into his heart; and they brought every man his present, vessels of silver, and vessels of gold, and raiment, harness and spices, horses and mules, a rate year by year." "And they brought unto Solomon horses out of Egypt, and out of all lands." And Solomon "made silver in Jerusalem as stones."

Finding no other great work at hand which demanded his immediate attention, he determined to go in person to Ezion-Geber, and build there a navy of ships which would compete with Hiram's, who had hitherto almost monopolized trade by navigation. Ezion-Geber was a seaport town on the northeastern extremity of the Red sea; and during David's life it had been conquered and kept in possession of the Israelites, to whom it was a place of great importance on account of its location upon a southern sea. For a hundred and fifty years it was retained, and then the Edomites, from whom it had been taken, recovered it. It was afterwards retaken by King Uzziah, who fortified it anew; but after a few years it fell into the hands of the Syrians, and then of the Romans and the Turks.

While it was owned by David, he commenced there a commercial intercourse with other nations; and now Solomon engaged skilful men of Hiram, and taking many of his own servants as workmen, went down in person to superintend his enterprise. The ships were no doubt made after the fashion of Hiram's, both in their construction and materials; for Solomon would not at that time be outdone in any undertaking, by a king of less notoriety and wealth. It was a great work and occupied much time, but at length the ships were finished and launched.

Hiram's men had peculiar skill in navigation; and they, with the assistance of a few Israelites

96   THE HISTORY OF KING SOLOMON.

whom Solomon wished to go in order to acquire
the art, manned the ships. It was gratifying to
the king to see that fleet, all his own, riding so
gracefully in the bay of Ezion-Geber, with its sails
unfurled to the breeze, ready to enter upon the
East India trade, where lay wealth untold; and

this is perhaps as ancient an authentic account of the trade, which has since enriched all nations who have entered upon it, as there is extant. The principal place of destination was the land of Ophir; the situation of which has been the subject of much unsatisfactory research, and which is conjectured by some to have been in the south of Africa, or Hindostan. Towards Ophir they set sail, while probably Solomon, his attendants, and many others, watched with enthusiastic feelings the retreating ships till they were lost to view. Three years must go by before they could again enter that port, and Solomon returned to Jerusalem.

The voyage was successful, and at the appointed time the ships returned to Ezion-Geber loaded with the riches and curiosities of the lands they had visited. Four hundred and fifty talents of gold were on board, estimated to have been worth over ten millions of dollars; besides this, there were silver and ivory and apes and peacocks; all of which

Solomon took to Jerusalem. This wealth greatly delighted the king; and no doubt the strange animals and birds were placed in his gardens, where they served to amuse not only the inmates and guests of the palace, but also the visitors from countries where such creatures were unknown.

Great risks were then run by sailing without compass or chart with such vessels through unknown seas; but voyage after voyage was made with great perseverance, and like results. Children with never-dying souls should, in the voyage of life, be willing to overcome every obstacle to gain those durable riches which shall be valuable long after this world and its scenes are swallowed up in eternity. Let us lay up treasures in heaven, for where our treasure is, there will our hearts be also.

CHAPTER IX.

THE VISIT OF THE QUEEN OF SHEBA—GOD IS ANGRY WITH SOLOMON.

Traders from all parts of the then known world were, for commercial purposes, passing to and from Palestine, which had now arrived at the zenith of its glory; and they saw with astonishment the dazzling splendor of the king, the immense wealth at his command, and the vast works which he had made. But their amazement was greatly increased by the wisdom of his proverbs and the beauty of his songs, which his subjects no doubt were proud to repeat to all foreigners of note who visited their country. Josephus says that Solomon sent riddles to Hiram, with the understanding that if they were not solved, certain sums of money should be returned; and that Solomon received great sums in this way. Hiram, in return, propounded riddles which Solomon failed to unravel, and consequently was obliged to return part of the money he had received. If this be true, and the riddles were made public, as they very likely were, much interest would be felt in their solution, even by the foreigners who visited the country. When the travellers returned home, these things would form the subject of their conversation, and thus the fame of Solomon spread far and near.

An intelligent and inquisitive queen, who lived probably in southern Arabia, or perhaps in Africa, heard her subjects talking of the wonders they had seen and heard in Palestine, and did not believe their reports; but she determined to go up and learn the truth of the matter, and test King Solomon's wisdom by hard questions of her own.

Dr. Scott thinks this queen was a descendant of Abraham by Keturah, and had some knowledge of the God of her fathers; and that it was upon this subject that she wished to question Solomon. Taking a great company of courtiers and attendants, with many camels laden with gold and precious stones, she left her home of comfort and plenty, to endure the fatigues of the long and toilsome journey.

At length she reached her place of destination; the gates were thrown open, and this queen and her very great train entered the far-famed city of Jerusalem. Solomon, dressed in his royal robes, received and entertained her according to her rank and dignity.

The gorgeous temple with its worship, and rich in its religious teachings, was to her particularly interesting; for, it was the shrine of Jehovah, with whom Solomon's fame was so closely connected; and all her hard questions in regard to the requirements, character, and worship of God, Solomon readily answered, to her great surprise and joy.

102   THE HISTORY OF KING SOLOMON.

She dined at his palace, where the dishes were of pure gold, and was amazed at the house he had built and the provisions of his table, "and the sitting of his servants, and the attendance of his ministers, and their apparel; and his cup-bearers, and his ascent by which he went up into the house of the Lord." He showed her his great ivory throne and his gardens and orchards, and his golden shields which hung in the house of Lebanon, and his chariots and horsemen. She probably saw Rehoboam, who was brought up in all this luxury, and who was heir to the wealth and glory which surrounded him.

She may have also seen many of the beautiful wives of Solomon, and listened in silent wonder to the sweet strains of music which floated through the long corridors of this magnificent palace. The whole was overpowering to her senses. and she found no words in which to express her overwhelming astonishment.

At length she exclaimed, "It was a true report that I heard in my own land of thine arts and of thy wisdom! Howbeit I believed not the words until I came and mine eyes had seen it; and behold, the half was not told me! thy wisdom and prosperity exceedeth the fame which I heard. Happy are thy men, happy are these thy servants which stand continually before thee, and that hear thy wisdom. Blessed be the Lord thy God which delighted in thee, to set thee on the throne of Israel; because the Lord loved Israel for ever, therefore made he thee king, to do judgment and justice."

When monarchs visited each other in that age of the world, it was their custom to give presents, according to their wealth and rank; and this queen now ordered hers to be brought to King Solomon. The first offering was the gold—one hundred and twenty talents—estimated as over two and a half millions of dollars.

This was truly a magnificent present; but after it, she gave a very great quantity of aromatic spices, such as Solomon never before or afterwards received. That kind did not grow in Palestine, neither was it much imported; it was therefore to him of great value.

After this she opened her caskets of precious stones, which were radiant and sparkling in their beauty, and gave them to the king.

VISIT OF THE QUEEN OF SHEBA. 105

Solomon was of course very much pleased with her gifts, and encouraged her to say what there was among his treasures that would be new or desirable to her; and whatever she selected or expressed a wish to possess, that he freely gave her; and when she would no longer choose, he of his own accord presented her a vast amount of his royal bounty.

Her visit being ended, she called together her retinue, took leave of the king, and returned to her native country greatly delighted with all she had seen and heard; and she carried home a report which far exceeded in its marvellous character that which had preceded her visit.

While these things were transpiring, other people were arriving from different parts of the earth, bringing gold, silver, and precious stones; and Solomon's ships were unloading upon his shores an abundance of the products of foreign countries. Among these were almug-trees, a valuable wood, out of which he made pillars and terraces for his palace and the temple; besides psalteries, harps, and all kinds of musical instruments. It is not now exactly known what this coral-wood was, but Solomon put it to such uses as would be likely to preserve it to posterity, for no such wood had ever before been seen in Palestine.

In one year there came to Solomon six hundred and sixty-six talents of gold, which was over sixteen millions of dollars; "besides what he had of merchantmen, and traffickers in spices, and of all the kings of Arabia, and of the governors of the country." Thus gold became so plenty that silver was of no account. Solomon had also a navy, which, with Hiram's, visited Tarshish, and returned every three years bringing gold and silver, ivory and apes, and peacocks.

Among the imports which came from Egypt was linen yarn. Some may imagine that this was not equal to that which is spun at this day; but those who have examined the linen cloth which is now found upon Egyptian mummies that were buried before Solomon's day, will acknowledge it to be equal perhaps to the finest of later years.

Pharaoh seems to have carried on a profitable trade with Solomon, his son-in-law, to the exclusion of other persons; and the price of whatever was taken was fixed by contract. Thus a good chariot horse could be had for about seventy-five dollars, and a chariot for three hundred dollars; and whatever Solomon received more than he wanted for his own use, was readily disposed of to the surrounding kings at large prices.

Josephus says that "Solomon had twenty-two thousand horses, and that they were very much exercised, that they might run swiftly and make a fine appearance; and that they exceeded all others for beauty. Their riders were young men noted for their size; and being tall and dressed in Syrian purple, with their "hair like Absalom's," hanging down their backs and sprinkled with gold, they

THE HISTORY OF KING SOLOMON.

made a very imposing and sparkling appearance. Each one had his bows and armor fitted to him. Solomon, dressed in white, and seated high in his chariot, often rode in the morning in the midst of these horsemen or a part of them, to a place about six miles from Jerusalem, where were fine gardens and rivulets of water."

Some of my young readers may by this time be quite astonished at the vast wealth, power, and display of Solomon; and ready to exclaim, that if they were as rich, they would do a great deal of good, and make every one around them happy. Many young and older people have had the same feelings before, when looking upon those far above them in wealth; but when wealth comes, it seems to clog up their good intentions and make the heart as cold and hard as the gold it loves. When money does this it is a curse, and we had better remain poor, and do what good we can by kind words and loving acts. If Solomon had remained in the moderate circumstances he was in when named Jedidiah, his life might have borne more testimony to the declaration that he loved the Lord; and his influence would then have been better over his son Rehoboam, who was growing up proud, arrogant, and self-willed; and it will not be surprising if we find him in after life a weak and wicked king.

During all the intoxicating prosperity which filled Solomon's reign, we see him struggling, though feebly, against the tide of sinful influences which dash against the weak barriers his conscience opposes; and we hear him despairingly exclaim, "I said, I will be wise; but it was far from me."

He had placed his feet upon the ground against which God had warned him, and as age advanced he gave fearful indications of an utter fall. The eyes of the world were upon him, for he had been renowned for his piety as well as for wisdom and wealth, and had built a house for the Great Jehovah, whom he assured Hiram that the heaven of heavens could not contain; and now, will he, who has been employed as an inspired writer, and who has given such wise and excellent warnings to others, apostatize and fall down before stocks and stones, the work of men's hands, and worship?

Poor human nature is the same in all ages of the world; and the injunction of our Saviour, "Watch and pray, lest ye enter into temptation," cannot be too closely followed and obeyed by the blood-bought souls of earth.

Solomon declared that he had denied himself nothing which his eyes desired; but in thus indulging his fancies, he had gone directly contrary to the express command of God. He loved and married many foreign women, together with the daughter of Pharaoh; "Women of the Moabites, Ammonites, Edomites, Zidonians, and Hittites, of the nations concerning which the Lord said unto the children of Israel, Ye shall not go in to them, neither shall they come in unto you; for surely they will turn away your heart after their gods." Yet Solomon married seven hundred of them, and they did turn away his heart, as the Lord had said.

It is not a little surprising that Solomon should have gone to other lands for wives, when the women of Palestine were worshippers at the temple, and also noted for their beauty. He may have succeeded in proselyting Pharaoh's daughter, for we hear of no temples erected for the gods of Egypt; and if so, he may have hoped to convert to his faith all whom he might gather into his palace. Many, even in this day, found their marriage relations upon similar hopes, but generally find, like Solomon, that instead of influencing their partners, they themselves are the losers. It is said that Solomon not only built a place of worship for Chemosh, the abomination of Moab, on the hill that is east of Jerusalem, and for Moloch, the abomination of the children of Ammon, of which we have already spoken, but did the same for all his wives, who burned incense and sacrificed unto their gods.

It is not at all surprising that the women who had the power to lead the king thus far, should succeed in after years in inducing him to accompany them into their temples, when they prostrated

GOD IS ANGRY WITH SOLOMON.

themselves in heathenish worship before their senseless images. Solomon no doubt felt when he married his Egyptian wife, that he was capable of self-control, and should never be led by her to forsake his God; and perhaps he might have stood, had that influence remained single; but when the door of our hearts is opened for one sin, it always stands ajar, and under one pretext and another, other sins enter; till finally, unless God rescues us, they take the reins of our wills and drive us where they please. This frequently was Solomon's condition when he was between fifty and fifty-five years of age. He had forfeited the promise of a long life, and was now rapidly approaching that long home whence no traveller returns; yet if he did not bow in worship to heathen deities, he countenanced by his presence this worship in others. Truly, the world would not call him bigoted, or illiberal in his views, as it does those who rigidly maintain their own ideas of right and wrong; but on the contrary, probably applauded his course, and followed his example. But God seeth not as man seeth, and he cannot look upon sin with any degree of allowance; Solomon's course was open before him, and his anger was kindled.

CHAPTER X.

SOLOMON'S TROUBLES—HIS ENEMIES, HADAD AND REZON—AHIJAH THE PROPHET, AND JEROBOAM—SOLOMON'S DEATH.

It is a dreadful thing to have the great God angry with us, yet the Bible says "he is angry with the wicked every day;" and as we are all sinners and constantly doing the things we should not, we have great reason to fear that his anger is often kindled against us. Children must not get the impression that God's anger is like that which they manifest towards each other. Theirs is sinful, and passionate, and unreasonable; while God's is holy, and just, and always brings deserved punishment upon those who excite it.

Solomon had been educated by a good and pious

father, and understood what God required of him; yet, after he became a man he disregarded what he knew to be right, and sinned greatly. For a long time God bore with him, and waited for his repentance, yet Solomon for a time grew worse and worse.

Every thing with Solomon seemed to be as prosperous as usual, when a message from God startled and alarmed him. His conscience must have been quickly aroused, as the prophet Ahijah came to him, and said, "Thus saith the Lord: forasmuch as this is done of thee, and thou hast not kept my covenant and my statutes which I have commanded thee, I will surely rend the kingdom from thee, and will give it to thy servant."

Perhaps he was humbled before the Lord in view of the great calamity which his sin was about to bring upon him; for the Lord immediately told him, that for Jerusalem's sake and for David's sake, he would not do it till Rehoboam should come upon the throne. Solomon saw that God's forbearance was not for any thing which he had done, and that he was living wholly upon mercies bestowed for the sake of David his father; and if these views had the right effect upon him, he was humbled before God, even as we poor sinners should be, who are spared only for the sake of Christ.

About the time that Solomon received this message from the Lord, Hadad, a son of the conquered king of Edom, began, by various means, greatly to annoy and harass his southern borders.

While matters were in this condition at the south, warlike movements began to exhibit themselves at the north, by Rezon, who had escaped from Zobah many years before, when David conquered Hadadezer, its king, and was now, with his followers, located at Damascus. It is probable that he did not readily get possession of that city, for David put garrisons there during his life. At length, however, he seized it; and holding the Israelites in great abhorrence, he did all he could to molest and annoy them.

With the anger of the Lord resting upon him, and an enemy upon his right hand and upon his left, Solomon might have felt that it was better "to be of an humble spirit with the lowly, than to divide the spoil with the proud," as he had said in his proverbs.

With his many fenced cities, and chariots and horsemen, it would seem hardly possible that Hadad or Rezon should make much advance into the country without being routed; yet, as Solomon had declared, "there is no wisdom, nor understanding, nor counsel against the Lord," who accomplishes his designs, whether by few or by many. Solomon could do nothing to quiet or conquer the united forces of his enemies, and during the rest of his life, which was only four or five years, he was continually molested by their incursions.

About the same time, another foe was raised up

in Jeroboam, whom Solomon had befriended and appointed to a lucrative office. He was the son of a widow who resided in the land of Ephraim; and like most boys who are without a father, he was obliged to earn his own support by labor. The first we hear of him he is in Jerusalem assisting in the work of building Millo. Solomon, who was ever on the lookout for men of the right stamp for his service, saw the industry of the young man Jeroboam, and learning that he was not only faithful in the duties assigned him, but a man of great valor, promoted him to be overseer of the labors of the tribes of Manasseh and Ephraim, or as others suppose, over the tribute collected from these two tribes.

But Jeroboam could not bear prosperity; and being bold, aspiring, and unprincipled, he soon began to form plans of a seditious character against the king. This was probably done by encouraging the murmurs and discontent of the people on account of the burdens laid upon them; designing, no doubt, an open revolt whenever he could do so safely.

While these things were occurring, the word of the Lord came to Ahijah, a prophet far advanced in life, who lived up in Shiloh, a city in Ephraim, and ordered him to go to Jeroboam with a message. The good prophet immediately obeyed, and started for Jerusalem; but before he reached it, he met Jeroboam in the fields dressed in a new coat, which Ahijah immediately seized and tore into twelve pieces. Jeroboam, understanding that the prophet was about to communicate some important message from God, quietly submitted to this harsh usage and awaited the result.

Taking up ten pieces and handing them to Jeroboam, he commanded him to take them, which he did; then the prophet said, "Thus saith the Lord, the God of Israel: Behold, I will rend the kingdom out of the hand of Solomon, and will give ten tribes

JEROBOAM.

to thee. But he shall have one tribe for my servant David's sake. And it shall be, if thou wilt hearken unto all I command thee, and wilt walk in my ways, and do that is right in my sight, to keep my statutes and my commandments, as David my servant did, that I will be with thee, and build thee a sure house, as I built for David, and will give Israel to thee."

The reason which Ahijah gave for this division of the nation was, that the people had gone after those heathen gods which Solomon had set up, and had worshipped them. This they had done in part through the bad example of their sovereign; and although Solomon was the greater sinner, they were guilty for following in his footsteps, and probably going beyond him in sin. It is no excuse for us, when wicked, that others have tempted us, and done the same things, for every man shall stand or fall before his own master. God had promised many things to David, and he regarded his word, and determined that the king's descendants should still be illustrious, and preserve the true light in Jerusalem.

Jeroboam had long desired the kingdom, and now that there was a certainty of his possessing it, he had as little care for his torn garment, as he had for the principles of right and wrong. David once had the promise of the kingdom, yet he would do nothing which would injure Saul, although he was constantly seeking David's life. Jeroboam, on the contrary, began to be so open in his rebellion, that Solomon was alarmed, and gave orders to arrest and put him to death. Jeroboam soon heard that the order had gone out, and slyly left the country. It was afterwards learned that he was in Egypt, under the care of Shishak the king. If Pharaoh had still been alive, Solomon could have requested him to put Jeroboam to death; but he was probably in the grave, and Shishak had no more regard for the king of Israel than for any other man.

Perhaps Jeroboam told Shishak that he had the promise of ruling over ten tribes, as soon as Solomon, who was now old and infirm, should die; and that may have been a reason why the king treated him with so much attention and respect. They undoubtedly had long and interesting conversations together in regard to the temple, the amount of gold expended upon the interior and upon the furniture, and upon those five hundred gold shields, which were hanging in the house of Lebanon; and it is not improbable that Shishak even then had a faint hope of making all this wealth his own, not many years thence.

Jeroboam would not at that time wish to excite any such feelings in the Egyptian king, for he expected, with his crown, to take a large share of the wealth of the country; but in after years, when Rehoboam became his open enemy, Jeroboam may have intimated to Shishak that Rehoboam might be easily conquered, and his country pillaged; for only five years after Solomon's death, Shishak came against Jerusalem with twelve hundred chariots, sixty thousand horsemen, and a numberless amount of footmen, and took the city. Every thing of value in the temple and palace, even all the gold dishes, candlesticks, and shields, he packed up and carried off to Egypt.

It is supposed that the perplexities by which

SOLOMON'S DEATH.

Solomon was surrounded in his last days, served to show him the folly of his former course, and to lead him to serve God again with his whole heart. This is probably true, for he evidently wrote the book of Ecclesiastes when taking a retrospective view of his life; and with a heart fully impressed with the unsatisfying nature of every earthly thing he had gained to himself, he abruptly exclaims, "Vanity of vanities, all is vanity!" He had labored for worldly pleasure and happiness, and it had proved nothing but "vexation of spirit."

He was now sixty years old, with every indication that the door of another world would soon open to receive and shut him for ever from the scene of all his earthly labors; and while he lingers upon the threshold, see him, with compassionate looks, beseechingly saying to you, "Remember now thy Creator in the days of thy youth, while the evil days come not, nor the years draw nigh, when thou shalt say, 'I have no pleasure in them.'" He had tried the experiment and found it hard to live in opposition to the direct commands of God; so he gives you, my young friends, this timely warning, that you may escape the misery that he suffered.

To Rehoboam and all other young men who are taking similar courses, he said, "Rejoice, O young man, in thy youth, and let thy heart cheer thee in the days of thy youth, and walk in the ways of thy heart and in the sight of thine eyes; but know thou, that for all these things God will bring thee into judgment." And his advice was, that if they wished to put sorrow from their hearts, they must put evil from their lives.

But hark! a few more words come floating back to us from the portals of the grave, and we hear him saying, "Hear the conclusion of the whole matter: Fear God and keep his commandments, for this is the whole duty of man; for God shall bring every work into judgment with every secret thing, whether it be good or whether it be evil."

SOLOMON'S DEATH.

Forty years Solomon had been king, but neither his riches, wealth, nor wisdom could retain the spirit when the angel of death came; and Solomon was obliged to yield to his power. No doubt every body, except a party of restless spirits, who complained of a heavy yoke and hard service, was alarmed when the news spread that the king was near his death; and every thing that friends or money could do was quickly tried. But it was of no use; God was calling for his spirit, and he must go. His great and splendid palace was vanity to him now, and his numerous wives with their heathen gods could give him no comfort. His complicity with their idolatries, we doubt not, filled him with bitter regrets; but he had confessed and forsaken his sins, and found mercy, and now in his last hours committed his soul to the God of David his father; and for the sake of Christ the Saviour to come, he was heard and saved.

Had we visited the palace a few days afterwards, we should have seen this great and wise man lying dead, and dressed for the grave. His work was done, and his friends carried him to the resting-place of his fathers, and buried him for ever from sight.

Never, never forsake the God who made you, but work in his cause as long as you live; for

"Oh, there's joy in rightly doing,
Never found in vice or sin;
Then obey a risen Saviour,
If a home in heaven you'd win.
Read the Bible; it will point you
To bright scenes of bliss on high,
Where there's rest for all the weary,
And our loved ones never die."

www.ingramcontent.com/pod-product-compliance
Lightning Source LLC
Chambersburg PA
CBHW020122170426
43199CB00009B/601